Ripley's Believe It or Not!

WEIRD-ITIES!

Publisher Anne Marshall
Editorial Director Rebecca Miles
Assistant Editor Charlotte Howell
Text Geoff Tibballs
Proofreader Judy Barratt
Picture Researchers James Proud, Charlotte Howell
Indexer Hilary Bird
Art Director Sam South
Senior Designer Michelle Foster
Reprographics Juice Creative

Executive Vice President Norm Deska
Vice President, Archives and Exhibits Edward Meyer

PUBLISHER'S NOTE

While every effort has been made to verify the accuracy of the entries in this book, the Publishers cannot be held responsible for any errors contained in the work. They would be glad to receive any information from readers.

WARNING

Some of the stunts and activities in this book are undertaken by experts and should not be attempted by anyone without adequate training and supervision.

Published by Ripley Publishing 2013
Ripley Publishing, Suite 188, 7576 Kingspointe Parkway, Orlando, Florida 32819, USA

2 4 6 8 10 9 7 5 3 1

ISBN 978-1-60991-025-9

Some of this material first appeared in *Ripley's Believe It or Not! Expect... The Unexpected*

Library of Congress Cataloging-in-Publication data is available

Manufactured in China in July/2013
1st printing

Ripley's Believe It or Not!

WEIRD-ITIES!

STRANGE WORLD

RIPLEY PUBLISHING

a Jim Pattison Company

STRANGE WORLD

On another planet. If you already thought the world was a bit mad, you'll think it's totally crazy when you get a load of this book! Read about the elephant with two trunks, the boa constrictor that appeared in a toilet, and the spooky glow-in-the-dark gravestone.

PAGE
36

PAGE
43

CRAZY HORSE

The detailed face of Crazy Horse stands 87 ft 6 in (26.7 m) high and took 50 years to complete—the lips alone took two years and the nose is 27 ft (8.2 m) long!

More than 8 million tons of rock has been blasted from a South Dakota mountain to create a sculpture depicting Native American chief Crazy Horse, who led the Oglala Sioux at the battle of the Little Bighorn in 1876. At the invitation of local Indian leaders, Boston-born sculptor Korczak Ziolkowski began work on Thunderhead Mountain back in 1948.

The crew uses precision explosive engineering to remove and shape mountain rock, the explosives being loaded into holes drilled to a depth of 35 ft (11 m). The final surface is smoothed by a jet torch, which operates at 3,300°F (1,815°C).

With the face complete, work is now progressing on the horse's head, which will stand 219 ft (66.7 m) high—the equivalent of a staggering 22 stories—and for which another 4 million tons of granite must be removed.

The final memorial will also feature a poem written by Ziolkowski, which will be carved into the hard mountain rock in letters 3 ft (0.9 m) tall.

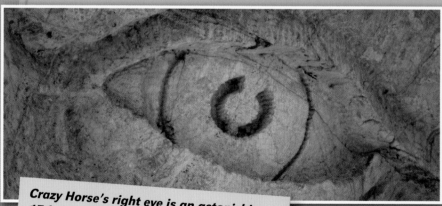

Crazy Horse's right eye is an astonishing 17 ft 9 in (5.2 m 23 cm) wide and reaches a whopping 8 ft 8 in (2.4 m 20 cm) in height.

HERCULEAN HOME

Jim Ryan lived in a giant redwood tree called "Hercules," near Dyerville, California. His house had one large circular room that measured 15 ft (4.6 m) in diameter.

BIG BOOT

A cowboy boot, 39 ft (12 m) tall and weighing 40 tons, looms over Edmonton, Alberta. It was built to promote the Western Boot Factory in 1989, at a cost of $200,000.

ROOFTOP GOATS

A store at Coombs, on Vancouver Island, British Columbia, has goats on the roof! They stay up there during the summer but come down for the winter.

SWIMMING IN BEER

In 2005, an Austrian holiday resort offered guests the chance to swim in a pool of beer. The resort, at Starkenberger in the Tyrol, filled seven pools with around 42,000 pt (20,000 l) of beer, claiming that beer helps to heal a variety of skin diseases.

GREEN MONUMENT

In 1971, when war broke out with Pakistan, archeologists in India draped the famous Taj Mahal monument with green cloth to try to camouflage it.

EYE SURGERY

Dr. Agarwal's eye hospital in Chennai, Bangalore, India, is shaped like a human eye.

OLD STAIRS

Archeologists in Hallstatt, Austria, have discovered an ancient wooden staircase, which was preserved in a salt mine, and is more than 3,000 years old.

SCENTED FOOD

An Argentinean restaurant has started adding designer perfumes to its dishes. Sifones and Dragones, in Buenos Aires, calls its cuisine Pop Food. The menu includes oysters flavored with Anaïs Anaïs, and Chanel No.5 ice cream.

BATMAN HOTEL

At the Hilton, Buenos Aires, Argentina, you can stay in a replica of the Batcave! The room is dedicated to Batman and there is even a secret passage leading from the "cave" to the next room.

NAKED TRUTH

To promote its art exhibition The Naked Truth, the Leopold Museum in Vienna, Austria, announced in 2005 that it was offering free admission to anyone who turned up in the nude!

TINY PUB

An old-style red telephone kiosk in Huddersfield, England, was converted into a tiny public bar.

RADIO STORE

Built to resemble an Atwater-Kent radio (c.1935), this storefront, in Niles, Michigan, measured 14 ft (4.3 m) high, 9 ft (2.7 m) wide, and 5 ft (1.5 m) deep.

TWO-TRUNKED!

Ripley's took possession of this preserved head in August 2005—the elephant itself had been shot in Zimbabwe on November 9, 2004. It is estimated that the animal was about five years old. The head was preserved, and DNA analysis has determined that the two trunks contain identical DNA patterns and that they were indeed from the same animal.

REVOLVING JAIL

At Council Bluffs, Iowa, is a curious three-story jail known as the Squirrel Cage. Built in 1885, the cells used to revolve constantly so the jailer could keep an eye on his prisoners at all times.

SNAIL MAIL

A letter sent to the German town of Ostheim-vor-der-Rhoen in 1718 arrived in 2004, surviving 286 years in the postal system.

THE KING'S STAMP

The king of rock 'n' roll, Elvis Presley, is the only person whose image appears on a U.S. postage stamp approved by a public vote.

TREE HOTEL

The Hotel Woodpecker, Vasteras, Sweden, sits 43 ft (13 m) above ground in an oak tree in the middle of a park. To reach their rooms, guests must climb a ladder (which is then removed) and meals are served via a basket attached to a pulley.

LUXURY CAVE

Kokopelli's Cave Bed and Breakfast is surely the world's most luxurious cave. Carved into the side of a mountain in Farmington, New Mexico, the cave covers 1,650 sq ft (153 sq m) and has every modern convenience for guests, including hot and cold running water, carpets, and even a kitchen.

CROSS GARDEN

William C. Rice, who died in 2004, erected hundreds of crosses on his land at Prattville, Alabama. It took him more than 20 years to create his garden of faith. Beside the crosses he painted messages of redemption on recycled window air-conditioner covers, refrigerator doors, and auto parts.

STATE VIEW

On a clear day you can see five states from the top of the Empire State Building in New York City—New York State, New Jersey, Connecticut, Massachusetts, and Pennsylvania.

TRANS-AUSTRALIAN SWIM

A group of 60 swimmers swam their way across Australia in a pool attached to the back of a truck traveling at 56 mph (90 km/h).

PETRIFIED DOG

Loggers at Waycross, Georgia, looked inside a hollow tree—and found a mummified dog. It was thought the dog had died after getting stuck in the tree, probably 20 years earlier. The petrified dog is now a local tourist attraction and is displayed inside a cross-section of log.

WHEEL OF FIRE

In 1928, a windmill on a farm in Kaltendorf, Germany, began spinning so fast in high winds that it eventually caught fire and burned to the ground.

PARK AND PRAY

Daytona Beach, Florida, boasts its own drive-through church. The congregation park their cars and then listen to sermons delivered from a balcony. During choral songs, some motorists toot their horns instead of clapping.

INN-CREDIBLE!

The town of Stafford, in England, lost an entire pub! Workmen dismantled the historic White Lion Inn in 1978 to make way for a new road, but forgot the storage location.

COUNTRY FOR RENT

Located in the Swiss Alps, the entire country of Liechtenstein (with an area of 62 sq mi/ 160 sq km) can be rented for corporate conferences.

WEIRD LAWS

In Sadieville, Kentucky, property owners are banned by law from mowing their lawns, but fishing in the nude is legal.

ON THE LINE

Norwegian slackliner Eiliv Ruud walks across crevasses and canyons thousands of feet above the ground—balancing on a moving rope that is 1 in (2.5 cm) wide.

How did you discover slacklining?

"I'm a professional mountain guide, and climb all over the world. In 1999 in Australia I saw some climbers who had strung a climbing rope between two trees and were balancing on it—a rest day activity. The line, or webbing, is about an inch wide, or less— it's called a slackline because it's not taut. It bounces and sways when you step onto it."

What is a highline?

"It's a slackline that is fixed much higher off the ground. Slacklining was started by American climbers in the late 1980s, although similar acts have been going on in circuses for years. The only difference between walking a low slackline and a highline is a mental one—it's all in your head."

Where did you do your first highline?

"My first one was across a crevasse on a glacier in Chamonix, France. On a high one like that, I have to empty my head of all thoughts—if you're not totally in the moment you will fall off. Highlining is almost like meditation. The lowline is more gymnastic—you can do more because you're not afraid to fall off."

What is the highest line you have ever walked?

"I did the Lost Arrow Spire in California's Yosemite National Park. It was 20 m long and 1,000 m high, and the rigging took us two days to put up. I don't think highlining has been done anywhere higher. I had been training on the same length line lower down and was completely comfortable, but when I first stepped onto it up there my feet just wobbled. I could barely stand, but I kept trying and eventually did it. That was a big one."

How do you train and prepare?

"You can learn the basics of slacklining in a couple of days—after that, it's just practice. The only training for the high ones is mental. You have to be confident in your skills. Before a highline walk I check the rigging, and check it again."

Have you ever lost your concentration or your balance?

"I've started to relax too soon and thought 'Oh I'm almost across now' and then lost it.

People do tricks like going backwards, turns, sitting or lying down on their backs, even back flips and handstands, but you still have to really concentrate—if you don't you'll just get halfway across and get thrown off."

What is the worst thing that could happen on a highline?

"If you don't do the rigging properly, the equipment could fail! On a highline, the results could be fatal. If I fall, I usually catch myself with the crook of my knee on the line and hang upside down. You actually get more injuries from the low lines because they bounce and can turn you upside down onto your head."

Is there anywhere you still want to do a highline?

"I would love to do a highline between the spires on the 3500-ft Troll Wall in Norway. But it doesn't matter really where you do it, as long as you are having fun. I've done it over lakes, rivers, glaciers, canyons, and across waterfalls. Being out in nature surrounded by magnificent scenery is an important part of the experience. But once you're high up on a difficult line you often don't pay much attention to the scenery, because you have to stay so focused on the task at hand."

DEM BONES DEM BONES

A chapel in the Czech Republic contains beautiful decorations and furnishings—and they're all made from human skeletons.

Centuries ago, the abbey at Sedlec was a major burial site. Around 1400, a church was built in the middle of the cemetery and a small chapel was used as an ossuary for the mass graves unearthed during construction. The task of exhuming skeletons and stacking their bones was given to a half-blind monk.

In 1870, wood-carver Frantisek Rint was employed by the Schwarzenberg family, who owned the church, to put the bone heaps in order. He turned 40,000 skeletons into amazing artistic creations, producing crosses, columns, and chalices of bone. From the center of the nave hangs an enormous chandelier featuring every bone in the human body several times over. Garlands of skulls drape the vaults, four bell-shaped bone mounds occupy the corners of the chapel, monstrances of bones flank the altar, and there is even a bone replica of the Schwarzenberg coat-of-arms.

The use of bones to create this and all the other decorations was intended to give the visitor an impression of the shortness of life and the inevitability of death.

Below is a detail from a pinnacle: a decorative pyramid of bones. Each pinnacle in the chapel is crowned with a cherub.

The bones come mainly from victims of the Black Death plague that swept across Europe in the 14th century, when 30,000 people were buried in Sedlec Cemetery. Some, however, are also casualties from the Hussite Wars of the 15th century— on some of the skulls the marks of battle wounds are clearly visible.

CLIMATE CHANGE

Mount Waialeale on the island of Kauai, Hawaii, often has 350 days of rain a year. Yet a few miles away at sea level, the annual rainfall is as low as 20 in (50 cm).

HIGHS AND LOWS

Mount Whitney, California, which is the highest peak in the U.S. outside Alaska, and Zabriskie Point in Death Valley, which is the lowest point in the U.S., are fewer than 80 mi (130 km) apart.

BARREL BOAT

Japanese sailor Kenichi Horie, aged 60, spent three months sailing alone across the Pacific Ocean on a yacht made out of beer kegs.

PEPPER SHAKERS

Some people collect stamps, others collect coins, but Andrea Ludden collects salt and pepper shakers. Her unusual 20-year obsession is displayed at the Salt and Pepper Museum in Gatlinburg, Tennessee. And with more than 17,000 shakers from all over the world, her collection is definitely not to be sneezed at!

TREE HUGGERS

If you thought climbing trees was only for small boys, think again. In August 2005, 52 tree-climbers from across the world scrambled up trunks at a staggering pace for the International Tree Climbing Competition in Nashville, Tennessee. Judging is strict, with penalties for unsafe maneuvers and bonuses for creativity, confidence, and use of equipment. The top prize of $1,000 went to the newly crowned world champions, Dan Krause, of Seattle, Washington, and Chrissy Spence, from New Zealand.

WINDMILL KING

Frank Medina was acknowledged as king of the windmills. He built up a collection of more than 2,000 windmills at Stockton, in California. At the age of 96, he also had all his own teeth and had never had a cavity!

RISKY OCCUPATION

An advertisement in the 1860s for the Pony Express Company read "must be expert riders, willing to risk death daily. Orphans preferred."

ICE SCULPTURE

Randy Finch, from Grand Rapids, Michigan, has built a double Ferris wheel out of ice—that actually works! The sculpture is made from more than 30 separate pieces of ice, most less than 1 in (2.5 cm) thick. Each of the individual carts turns on an ice axle. Finch has also made a full-sized ice pool table (right), complete with ice balls and cues.

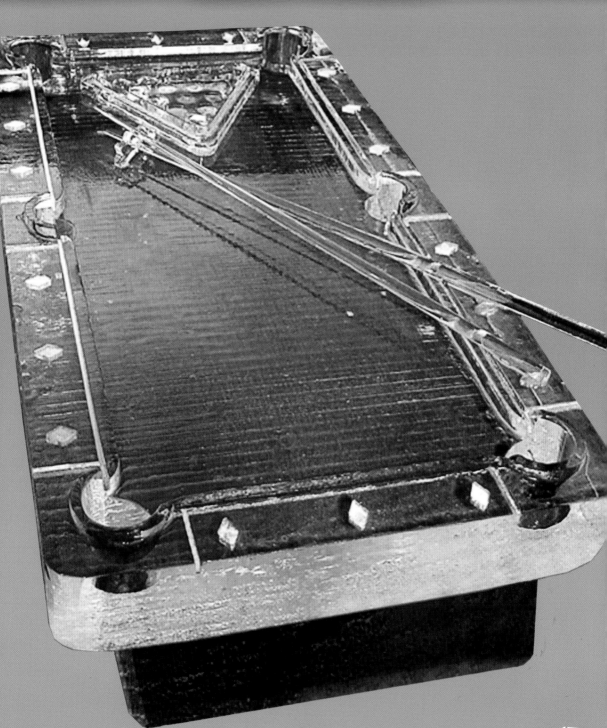

CAVE MUSIC

The Great Stalacpipe Organ, in the Luray Caverns of Virginia, is a gigantic musical instrument that covers 3.5 acres (1.4 ha). Invented in 1954, the organ uses natural stalactites instead of metal pipes to make beautiful music. Its inventor, mathematician and scientist Leland Sprinkle, walked the length of the caverns, deliberately choosing stalactites that would perfectly match the musical scale.

KICKING THE BOTTLE

Bottle Kicking (and Hare Pie Scrambling) competitions have taken place on Easter Monday in Leicestershire, England, since 1771. Yet this curious sport involves neither bottles nor kicking.

The contest—often bloody and brutal—takes place between the neighboring villages of Hallaton and Medbourne. The rival villagers fight over three small beer barrels and attempt to manhandle two of them over their opponents' line. The respective goal-lines are two streams a mile apart. The free-for-all has no other rules and the game can last for several hours.

LONG OVERDUE

Padma Maya Gurung, of Nepal, spent an extra six years in jail because a letter of release from the supreme court, issued in 1997, was lost in the mail.

COLORADO KEYS

The Baldpate Inn in Estes Park, Colorado, has more than 20,000 keys on display. The collection boasts keys from Mozart's wine cellar, the Pentagon, Westminster Abbey, and even Frankenstein's castle.

UNDERGROUND CHURCH

The amazing 750-year-old Church of St. George in the Ethiopian village of Lalibela is built vertically downward! It has been cut out of the rock in the shape of a cross and is surrounded by a trench. The top of the church is flush with ground level. There are ten other underground churches in the area, many connected by tunnels.

SYMBOLIC POT

Towering over the town of Davidson, Saskatchewan, is a coffee pot 24 ft (7.3 m) tall that could hold 150,000 8-oz (227-g) cups of coffee. The giant pot is intended as a symbol of Davidson's friendliness and hospitality.

PAPER PLANE MUSEUM

Kahului, Hawaii, is home to a museum devoted solely to paper airplanes. There are more than 2,000 models ranging from postage-stamp size to paper planes with wingspans of more than 6 ft (1.8 m).

UNEXPECTED GUESTS

Visitors to a luxury manor house in Kenya are likely to be joined at the dinner table by some unusual guests—a herd of giraffes! Set in 120 acres (49 ha) of forest on the outskirts of Nairobi, Giraffe Manor has welcomed the likes of Mick Jagger, Johnny Carson, Brooke Shields, and Lee Remick. But it is the rare Rothschilds' giraffes that have been the star attractions since moving in to the manor in 1974.

TREE VILLAGE

Believe it or not, the grounds of Alnwick Castle, England, are home to a remarkable tree house—or, rather, a 60-ft (18.3-m) high tree "village"— set among the branches of 16 lime trees. The brainchild of Jane, Duchess of Northumberland, it opened in January 2005, having cost more than £3.3 million ($6.7 million). There are five rooms, which include a restaurant, and 6,000 sq ft (557 sq m) of suspended walkways.

SEASONAL SNOWMAN

A smiling snowman, 35 ft (10.6 m) tall, stands near Beardmore, Ontario. Made of wood over a steel frame, the snowman was built in 1960 to promote the community and the local ski hill. He even dresses for the time of year—in summer he has sunglasses and a fishing pole; in winter he wears a scarf and carries a curling broom.

ON THE BORDER

The Hotel Arbez at Les Rousses straddles the French–Swiss border and offers guests a choice of rooms in either France or Switzerland.

MILLIONS OF BOOKS

There are more than 130 million items on bookshelves that measure around 530 mi (853 km) in length in the Library of Congress, Washington D.C.

FENCE FORTE

Musician Simon Dagg, from Kent, England, is so obsessed with his first love that he spent a whopping £60,000 ($105,000) fine-tuning the 120-ft (36.5-m) fence around his house so that it would play like a giant glockenspiel. He worked 12 hours a day for five years tuning the metal bars to play like the real thing.

BONE CABIN

Near Medicine Bay, Wyoming, is a cabin built entirely from dinosaur bones. Thomas Boylan began collecting discarded bone fragments from a nearby paleontological dig in 1916. Seventeen years later, he had managed to amass an amazing 5,796 bones, weighing a total of 102,116 lb (46,319 kg), which he then decided to use to construct a lodge measuring 29 ft (8.8 m) long and 19 ft (5.8 m) wide.

DUCK WALK

Carp collect in such numbers and at such a high density at the base of the spillway of the Pymatuning Reservoir near the town of Linesville, Pennsylvania, that ducks are able to walk across the backs of the fish and hardly get their feet wet!

UPSIDE-DOWN BED

Fancy sleeping in an Upside Down Room, where all the furniture is suspended from the ceiling and you sleep and sit in boxes beneath the floorboards? Or how about the Symbol Room (above), made from 300 square, wooden plates decorated with black-and-white symbols? What about the Coffin Room or the Padded Cell Room? Propeller Island City Lodge Hotel in Berlin, Germany, has 30 rooms, each with a unique, wacky theme.

HOUSE OF CLOCKS

In 1960, Ray Thougen rescued a grandfather clock from a garbage truck and bought three other junk clocks for $5. That was the start of a clock collection that now stands at almost a thousand pieces—all in full working order. For 17 years, Thougen lovingly restored damaged clocks, often without diagrams, before the collection was bought by Ray Sweeney in 1977. Unable to deny the passing of time, both Rays are now dead, but their legacy ticks on at the House of Clocks, in Waukon, Iowa.

DOG PADDLE

Among the 500 swimmers that competed in the South End Rowing Club's annual Alcatraz Invitational in 2005, one stood out—Jake the golden retriever. The only four-legged competitor in the field, Jake jumped from a boat near Alcatraz and swam 1.2 mi (1.9 km) to the San Francisco shoreline, finishing a creditable 72nd in the race.

MUD MOSQUE

The Grand Mosque Djenne in Mali is 328 ft (100 m) long and 131 ft (40 m) wide—and is made from mud!

HOME ON WHEELS

John Martie, a sightseer who lost his sight in an accident, built himself a house on his car and covered 50,000 mi (80,465 km) in the U.S.A.

SIMONE
JULY 22ND 1960
AGED 8 YEARS

WENDY
14 YEARS
AUG. 30TH
1953

SIMON
MAR. 2ND 1969.
AGED 5 YEARS.

GEMMA
10TH NOV. 2000
AGED 14 YEARS

ALEX
27TH DEC. 2001
AGED 10 YEARS

BUNGY
9TH MAY 1985

TRUSTY

JASMIN
22ND DEC.
2003
AGED 17 YRS.

TINA
SEPT. 1972.
12½ YEARS.

VICTORIA
25TH JUNE 1974.
AGED 14½.

MARK
30TH SEPT. 1974.
AGE 13½ YRS.

PET CEMETERY

Jean Pyke has buried 22 pets in her garden on Hayling Island in England. Alongside the pets are also buried the ashes of her dead husband.

ROADSIDE ODDITY

In 1930, to catch the eye of passing motorists, brothers Elmer and Henry Nickle built a roadside gas station at Powell, Tennessee—in the shape of an airplane. More recently the airplane building, complete with wings and a propeller, has been used as a car lot.

JUNK HOUSE

When eccentric sculptor Art Beal bought a hillside plot at Cambria, California, in 1928 he set about building a junk house. He spent 50 years realizing his dream and, as the town's garbage collector in the 1940s and 1950s, he used the junk he collected in the construction. He called the result Nitt Witt Ridge, Beal's alias being Captain Nitt Witt.

EASIER THAN ABC

Rotokas, a language of the South Pacific, has an alphabet with only 11 letters, comprising six consonants and five vowels.

WRECK REPLICA

The world's most bizarre Stonehenge replica can be found near Alliance, Nebraska, made entirely from wrecked cars. Built by Jim Reinders in 1987, "Carhenge" has 38 cars, positioned in a circle 96 ft (29 m) in diameter, echoing its famous English counterpart.

ELEPHANT HOTEL

In 1881, James T. Lafferty built a hotel in the shape of an elephant. Nicknamed Lucy, this historical landmark is now located in Margate, New Jersey. Lucy is 65 ft (19.8 m) tall and weighs 90 tons. For $4 you can wander through its pink rooms and get an elephant's-eye view of the city.

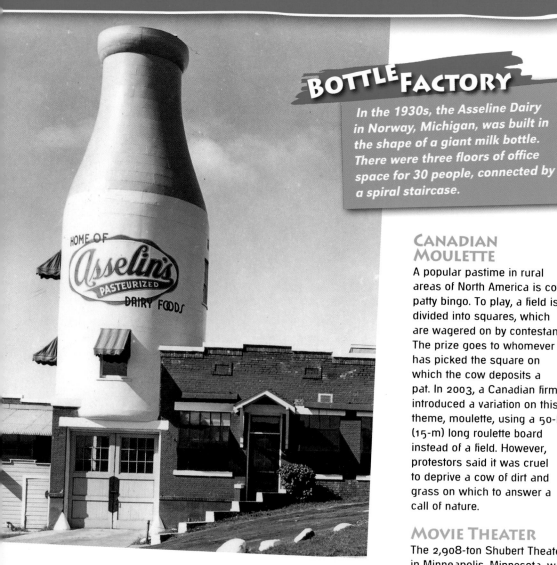

BOTTLE FACTORY

In the 1930s, the Asseline Dairy in Norway, Michigan, was built in the shape of a giant milk bottle. There were three floors of office space for 30 people, connected by a spiral staircase.

HOME OF
Asselin's
PASTEURIZED
DAIRY FOODS

CANADIAN MOULETTE

A popular pastime in rural areas of North America is cow patty bingo. To play, a field is divided into squares, which are wagered on by contestants. The prize goes to whomever has picked the square on which the cow deposits a pat. In 2003, a Canadian firm introduced a variation on this theme, moulette, using a 50-ft (15-m) long roulette board instead of a field. However, protestors said it was cruel to deprive a cow of dirt and grass on which to answer a call of nature.

MOVIE THEATER

The 2,908-ton Shubert Theater in Minneapolis, Minnesota, was moved in one piece to a new site three blocks away in 1999. The theater was transported on rubber wheels for a short journey that took 12 days.

PROPHETIC NAME

When Nancy Araya opened a new restaurant in Santiago, Chile, in 2005, she decided to call it Car Crash because the area was an accident blackspot. But within a few weeks the restaurant had to close after a passing car crashed through the entrance of the building.

LOBSTER DERBY

In a spoof of the Kentucky Derby, lobster racing takes place every May in Aiken, South Carolina, on a track called Lobster Downs. The track is a series of water-filled tanks where progress can be painfully slow. Indeed some lobsters have been known to die mid-race.

ICY WEATHER

Gale-force north-easterly winds brought freezing temperatures and freakish weather to Lake Geneva, Switzerland, in January 2005. With 70 mph (120 km/h) winds and temperatures of 10°F (−12°C), waves swept over the lake's banks and droplets of water froze instantly on everything they touched.

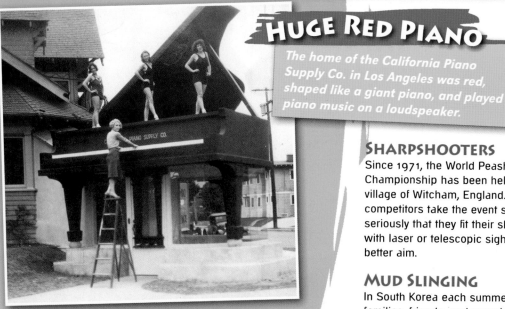

HUGE RED PIANO

The home of the California Piano Supply Co. in Los Angeles was red, shaped like a giant piano, and played piano music on a loudspeaker.

SHARPSHOOTERS

Since 1971, the World Peashooting Championship has been held in the village of Witcham, England. Some competitors take the event so seriously that they fit their shooters with laser or telescopic sights for a better aim.

MUD SLINGING

In South Korea each summer, families, friends, and complete strangers indulge in hours of mud slinging—and enjoy every minute of it. They are taking part in the annual Poryong Mud Festival, a mad, muddy mess that features mud baths, mud sculpture, mud body-painting, and even a mud beauty contest. Hundreds of willing competitors seize the opportunity to get grubby, encouraged by the beneficial minerals in the local mud, which are believed to reduce wrinkles and wash away excess oils from the skin.

QUICK SERVICE

At Lambert's Café, Sikeston, Missouri, they don't bring bread rolls in a basket—they throw them at you! One day in 1976, the restaurant was so busy that proprietor Norman Lambert was unable to get through the crowd to serve the rolls. A customer shouted, "Throw it!" and Lambert did—and the tradition began.

RED APPLE HOUSE

This apple-shaped restaurant lay on a dirt road in Missouri. It had windows all around, a chimney for a stem, and measured 30 ft (9 m) in height and 100 ft (30 m) in circumference.

MESSAGE IN A BOTTLE

William T. Mullen's wife warned him that if he didn't stop drinking she would humiliate him after his death. He paid no attention and died in 1863, whereupon she carried out her threat by giving him a gravestone—at Clayton, Alabama—in the shape of a whiskey bottle.

BARKING BEACH

Believe it or not, Barking Sands Beach, on the Hawaiian island of Kauai, has sand that barks like a dog! The dry sand grains emit this strange sound when you walk on them in bare feet.

CHOCOLATE MOOSE

Lenny the Moose is made from 1,700 lb (771 kg) of the finest milk chocolate! A life-sized chocolate moose, Lenny resides at Len Libby Handmade Candies in Scarborough, Maine. He was born in 1997 at the request of the store's co-owner Maureen Hemond, and created on-site in four weeks by local sculptor Zdeno Mayercak. The moose is 8 ft (2.4 m) tall and over 9 ft (2.7 m) from nose to tail. He began as a metal armature onto which 10-lb (4.5-kg) chocolate blocks were placed. Melted chocolate was then used as the mortar to hold the blocks together.

HOW MANY HOOVES?

This six-legged calf was born on a farm in Poland in February 2005. It belongs to farmer Jaroslaw Garbal, who has named the animal "Star."

MONKEY MAYOR

When the residents of Hartlepool, England, voted for a new mayor in 2002, they elected a man in a monkey costume! H'Angus the Monkey, mascot of the the town's soccer team, campaigned successfully with the slogan "free bananas for schoolchildren."

FROG RACE

Since 1946, Rayne, Louisiana, has hosted a Frog Derby. Girls from the town dress up frogs in jockey uniforms and encourage them to hop along a course.

FIREPROOF CITY

The Bolivian capital, La Paz, is very nearly fireproof. Located 12,000 ft (3,660 m) above sea level, there is barely enough oxygen in the air to support combustion.

PYRAMID HOUSE

Jim and Linda Onan wanted a house with a difference, so they created a six-story building shaped like a pyramid and made out of 24-carat gold plate. The Gold Pyramid, which is in Wadsworth, Illinois, has an interior that measures an enormous 17,000 sq ft (1,580 sq m). Furnished in the style of the ancient Egyptian pharaohs, it contains a replica of King Tutankhamen's tomb, while the grounds feature a triple-pyramid garage and a 64-ft (19.5-m) statue of the Egyptian king Ramses.

MAGNETIC HILL

Bizarrely, cars seem to roll uphill at Magnetic Hill, near Moncton, New Brunswick. The phenomenon was first noticed in the 19th century when farmers observed their horses straining to pull wagons down the hill, but when going uphill the wagons would bunch up at the horses' feet. Today, tourists drive their cars to the foot of the hill, stop, put them into neutral, and then coast backward, uphill.

THE GOAT KING

For three days a year, Ireland is ruled by a goat! Before the Puck Fair, held in Killorglin, Kerry, every August, chief goat-catcher Frank Joy heads into the hills and captures a wild mountain goat. The goat is duly crowned King Puck and placed on an elevated platform in the center of the town square where, from a height of 50 ft (15 m), he looks down on his subjects for the three-day duration of the fair.

SANDPAPER MUSEUM

Two Harbors, Minnesota, must be the only place in the world that has a museum devoted solely to sandpaper. The collection is located in the house of John Dwan, one of the founders of the 3M Company. As a special treat, visitors are given free sandpaper samples.

SHIP SHAPE

A car wash at Eau Claire, Wisconsin, is shaped like a cruise liner, complete with two smoke stacks.

HORN TREE

Believe it or not, at Junction, Texas, there is a Christmas tree made entirely from deer horns!

BANANA STAMP

There was once an official stamp issued by the country of Tonga (in the South Pacific) shaped like a banana.

TREE TUNNEL

You can drive through trees at Leggett, California. The bases of giant redwoods have been tunneled out so that cars can pass through.

SEWER CONSTRICTOR

In October 2005, in Manchester, England, a 10-ft (3-m) boa constrictor appeared in an apartment toilet bowl. A concrete block was placed on the toilet lid to prevent the snake escaping before firefighters and plumbers arrived. Using hi-tech fiber-optic equipment, they checked the sewage pipes, but could find no evidence of the snake. Another resident in the apartment building then captured the snake, having found it on his bathroom floor. The snake appeared to have been living happily in the apartments' sewage system!

CAR SPIKE

The parking lot at the Cermak Plaza Shopping Centre, Berwyn, Illinois, looks like the scene of a horrific accident—shoppers turn a corner to discover eight cars impaled on a 40-ft (12-m) spike! Luckily, it is only a sculpture, named "The Spindle," created by Californian artist Dustin Shuler, from Los Angeles, in 1989.

BACKWARD BIKING

Some people aren't satisfied with riding a bicycle the conventional way—they prefer to ride it backward. In this curious sport, the rider sits on the handlebars instead of the seat, facing backward, and peddling and steering in reverse! The bikes are not fitted with mirrors or any special adaptations. In 2002, Dutchman and expert backward-cyclist Pieter de Hart cycled an amazing 16.7 mi (26.9 km) in one hour.

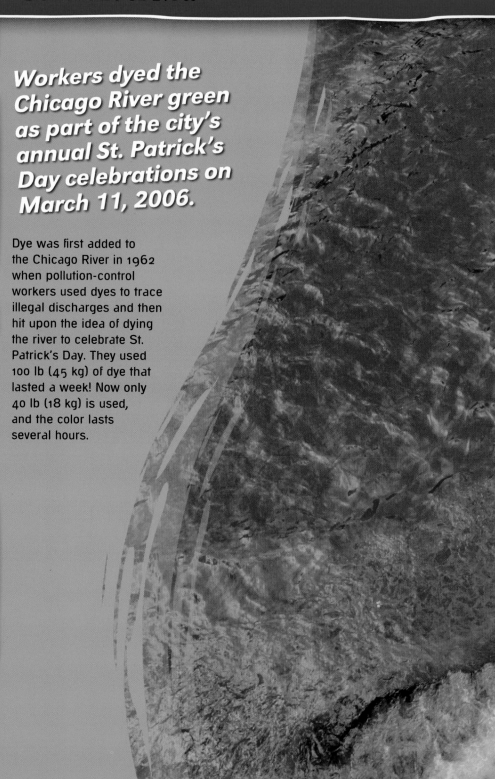

GREEN RIVER

Workers dyed the Chicago River green as part of the city's annual St. Patrick's Day celebrations on March 11, 2006.

Dye was first added to the Chicago River in 1962 when pollution-control workers used dyes to trace illegal discharges and then hit upon the idea of dying the river to celebrate St. Patrick's Day. They used 100 lb (45 kg) of dye that lasted a week! Now only 40 lb (18 kg) is used, and the color lasts several hours.

GONE TO POT

The site of the Sky Kingdom religious sect in Kampung Batu, Malaysia, was dominated, until its demolition in 2005, by a two-story building in the shape of a giant pink teapot. The teapot was apparently inspired by the dreams of one of the sect's followers.

DOLL HABIT

At Indian River, Michigan, is a museum with around 525 dolls, all dressed as nuns. The Cross in the Woods Nun Doll Museum is the brainchild of Sally Rogalski, who, as a young girl in 1945, used to dress her dolls in nuns' habits to preserve Catholic history. The Rogalskis received a special blessing from Pope John Paul II for their work "in helping to promote vocations to the priesthood and religious life through their doll collection."

BEER-CAN CASTLE

Faced with a growing pile of empty beer cans, Vietnam veteran Donald Espinoza from Anonito, Colorado, decided to put them to good use. He spent the following 25 years building a fortress—named Cano's Castle—from the cans, as well as from hubcaps and strips of aluminum.

A MEAL TOO FAR

A Burmese python 13 ft (4 m) long bit off more than it could chew when it tried to swallow whole a 6 ft (1.8 m) American alligator. Both animals were found dead, floating in the water. Experts think the alligator was still alive when the snake swallowed it snout first, and that repeated kicks from its hind legs ruptured the snake's stomach wall.

Large wads of alligator skin were found in what remained of the snake's stomach, and the alligator had also sustained wounds behind the eyes and on the shoulder. Until an alligator's spinal cord is severed, it can still move its legs, so its sharp claws could have torn through the snake's skin, causing the gaping hole.

After the snake died, its head was probably eaten by another alligator.

The alligator's tail and hind legs are protruding from a large hole where the python's body literally burst under the pressure of its meal! The stomach of the python still surrounds the head, shoulders, and forelimbs of the alligator.

BIG SMOKE

This giant cigar, made in Miami, Florida, in 1994, is 6 ft (1.8 m) long, 11 in (28 cm) in diameter, and weighs 55 lb (25 kg)—holding enough tobacco to make 3,000 regular no. 1-sized cigars! It took two men two weeks to hand roll.

DEEP SLEEP

Near Västerås, Sweden, is a hotel where guests sleep in an underwater room. The brainchild of artist Mikael Genberg, the bedroom at the Utter Inn is situated 10 ft (3 m) below the surface of Lake Mälaren, with a window offering a panoramic view of passing marine life.

FISH HOTEL

Chicago's newest downtown hotel caters solely for fish. This "fish hotel" is a series of small gardens densely planted with pondweed to satisfy the scaly inhabitants of the Chicago River. Some gardens are floating, others submerged, and all of the "rooms" are fitted with underwater cameras so that humans can catch a glimpse of the action.

TURTLE POWER

At Dunseith, North Dakota, a giant turtle has been welded together from more than 2,000 steel wheel rims. The head alone weighs more than a ton.

LOOK WHO'S TALKING

You never know who's talking to you at Vent Haven, as this museum at Fort Mitchell, Kentucky, is home to more than 600 ventriloquists' dummies. It is the legacy of W.S. Berger, who collected ventriloquism memorabilia from the early 20th century up until his death in 1972.

INDOOR BEACH

With 3,350 sq yd (2,800 sq m) of white sand, the Ocean Dome beach, at Miyazaki, Japan, is one of the world's finest. But what makes it unusual is that it is indoors. The beach features plastic palm trees that sway in an artificial breeze, and 13,500 tons of salt-free "sea." A machine creates surf up to 11 ft (3.4 m) high, and even when the giant roof is open the temperature is a warm 86°F (30°C). There's no danger of sunburn or shark attacks and even the surrounding volcanoes are fake. But perhaps the oddest thing about the dome is that the real beach and sea are only 300 yd (275 m) away!

FOAM HOME

At Centralia, Washington State, is a house covered in Styrofoam®™. The owner, former art teacher Richard Tracy, has been working on the house for more than 20 years.

REMOTE ISLAND

The uninhabited Bouvet Island in the South Atlantic is probably the world's most remote island. The nearest land—Queen Maud Land in Antarctica—is 1,050 mi (1,690 km) away, and is also uninhabited.

GIANT STAMP

In Cleveland, Ohio, stands a gigantic office rubber stamp. Made by artist Claes Oldenburg in 1985, the steel structure is 28 ft (8.5 m) tall and 48 ft (14.6 m) long.

GIANT CHAIR

A steel chair, 33 ft (10 m) high, stands next to a furniture store in Anniston, Alabama. Built in 1981, the structure can withstand winds of up to 85 mph (137 km/h).

DINING ON TOILETS

A family settle down to a meal in a toilet-themed restaurant named Martun ("toilet" in Chinese), in Kaohsiung, China. Diners sit on toilet seats and the food arrives in bowls shaped like Western-style toilets or Asian-style "squat pots."

LUXURY HEARSE

An Australian funeral director is offering a highly unusual hearse with its own minibar, DVD player, and fresh coffee-maker. The luxurious mint-green vehicle, which can be hired from Tobin Brothers of Melbourne, is fitted with chrome handrails, tinted windows, pop-out cup holders, and atmospheric lighting. It can hold up to 12 mourners and a coffin.

NOVELTY COFFINS

Coffin-maker Vic Fearn, from Nottingham, England, likes to offer a funeral with a difference. Mr. Fearn makes novelty coffins to cater for every taste and interest, in such diverse shapes as a sports bag, a kite, a canal boat, and a guitar.

DOLPHIN MYSTERY

In August 2003, locals reported a strange sighting on Florida's Gasparilla Lake—a dolphin. Yet the lake is totally landlocked, with no access to the Gulf of Mexico!

DUCK MARCH

Guests at the Peabody Hotel, Memphis, Tennessee, witness a truly strange ritual. Twice a day—at 11 a.m. and 5 p.m.—ducks march in a line from their rooftop penthouse to the hotel elevator and then travel down to the marble fountain situated in the hotel lobby. The Peabody Ducks have been a tradition for more than 70 years, dating back to when the hotel manager, Frank Shutt, returned from a drunken hunting trip and thought it would be fun to place some of his living decoy ducks in the hotel's fountain.

PRAYER MAIL

Every year, the Israeli post office in Jerusalem sorts up to 3,000 letters addressed to "God" and forwards them to the Western Wall, where they are inserted into the cracks at the holy site.

MIRACLE PUTT

There should be no cursing on a miniature golf course at Lexington, Kentucky—because the 54-hole course has a biblical theme throughout. The first 18 holes are based on events in the Old Testament, the second 18 are related to the New Testament, and the final 18 are the toughest—the miracles. Where else can you play through Jesus's tomb and Jonah's whale, or conquer Mount Sinai with a putter?

CLIMBING HIGH

For 40 years, this magnolia tree in Kent, Ohio, was used to train students of the Davey Tree Expert Co. No man graduated until he could climb the tree without spurs.

LONG PAYMENT

At one time, Filipinos could wear their hair long only if they paid a fee of 78 cents a year.

BIGGEST CAP

Visitors to Rocanville, Saskatchewan, may be amazed to find it is home to an enormous baseball cap. More than 13 times the regular size, it was built from fiberglass in 1988 and sits perched on top of a pole.

BATHTUB RACE

The summer of 2005 witnessed the 39th staging of one of Canada's strangest events—the Great International World Championship Bathtub Race, at Nanaimo on Vancouver Island. Motor-powered fiberglass bathtubs—some costing up to $3,000—take to the waters on a 36-mi (58-km) round course. When the race was held back in 1967, the sea was so choppy that only 47 of the 200 starters finished.

REINDEER PARKING

A hotel in the Siberian city of Nadym announced in March 2005 that it was offering free parking for reindeer! The hotel aimed to cash in on the area's major industry—reindeer breeding.

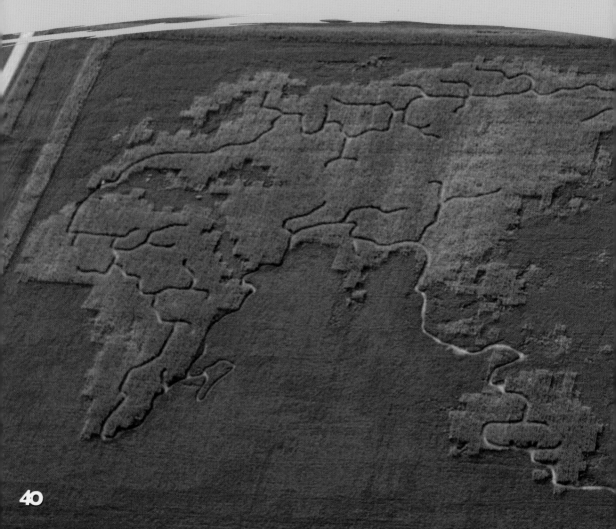

EXPENSIVE WIND

During the 18th century, in the village of Zaanse in the Netherlands, the government forced windmill owners to pay a tax on the wind.

FREE ELECTRICITY

John Lorenzen, of Woodward, Iowa, who has never paid for electricity, has run his 100-acre (40.5-ha) farm using windmills for more than 60 years.

PLANTING THE WORLD

For the last five years, Ernst and Nelly Hofer have planted a giant maze on their farm. In 2005, they planted a world map. Laid out with GPS, the landmasses are made from feed corn and the oceans are soybeans. One step or stride on the ground in the maze is equal to traveling 43 mi (69 km) on the Earth's surface—that means it would take just 54 strides to cover the breadth of America!

41

EIFFEL REPLICA

If you go to Paris, you expect to see the Eiffel Tower, but not one that is only 60 ft (18 m) tall. But that's what you'll find at Paris, Tennessee—a replica of the French original created by Dr. Tom Morrison using 6,000 steel rods and 500 pieces of Douglas fir. The American tower was originally on display at Christian Brothers University in Memphis, but in 1992 it was moved to Paris.

COSY RABBITS

William Schultz, of Grants Pass, Oregon, heats his greenhouse with the body heat of 350 caged rabbits!

ARMY DECOY

During World War II, the British magician Jasper Maskelyne was recruited to create an entire fake seaport to hide the Suez Canal and to disguise the activities of the army by building decoy troops. He acheived this amazing deception by using mirrors, flashing lights, and an array of wooden props.

DEAD ENDS

Alliance, Ohio, is the only town in the whole of the U.S.A. that has a main street that is a dead end at both of its ends.

PAPERWEIGHT MUSEUM

A museum at Cambridge, Ohio, boasts more than 4,000 paperweights. The Degenhart Paperweight Museum houses the collection of former glass-factory owner Elizabeth Degenhart, who picked up her paperweights between 1947 and her death in 1978.

GOING NOWHERE

Eccentric British tycoon Joseph Williamson dug a network of tunnels under the city of Liverpool, England, 200 years ago. Most of the tunnels lead nowhere.

MOUNTAIN JOB

In August 2005, executives of ImageNet Co. gave job applicants an initiative test by holding interviews at 12,388 ft (3,776 m) at the summit of Mount Fuji! They wanted to make sure that new employees would have what it takes to scale the heights of business.

DISH OF THE DAY

Most people cook beneath the hood of an oven, but Bob Blumer prefers cooking beneath the hood of a car. Hollywood's Surreal Gourmet, Blumer has championed cooking meat and fish in aluminum foil on car engines. His recipes often begin: "Preheat the engine for 20 miles..." He has also toured the U.S.A. promoting his unusual recipes in his "Toastermobile," a trailer equipped with a professional kitchen, and topped with two slices of toast, each 8 ft (2.4 m) high!

IN-FLIGHT CATERING

In Canada, a grounded airplane has been turned into a restaurant—Super Connie's Airplane Bar, in Mississauga, Ontario.

INVISIBLE BAR

For years, the town of Nothing lived up to its name. With a population of just four, it was nothing more than a gas station on Hwy 93 between Phoenix and Las Vegas. Then Ben Kenworthy decided to build an invisible bar. Drivers can't see the bar in daylight because the building is camouflaged by thousands of light bulbs, reducing it to a glitter in the Arizona Desert. Passersby can see the light, but assume it is just the sun's reflection.

MOVING LAND

The fastest-moving place on the Earth is the South Pacific island of Niuatoputapu. It is moving at a rate of 10 in (25 cm) a year.

SILENT MOURNING

Women of the Warramunga tribe of Australia do not speak for a year after the death of their husbands—communicating instead only with hand and arm gestures.

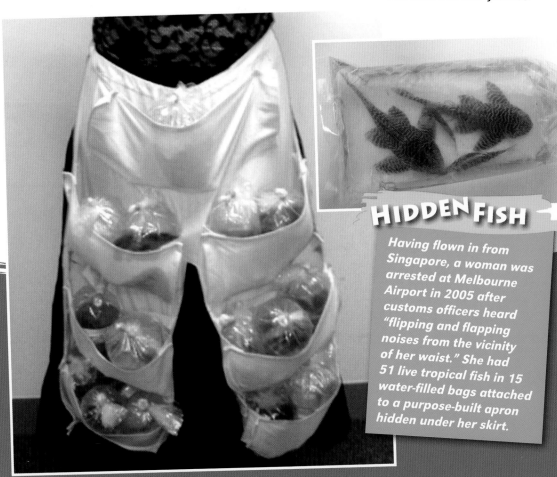

HIDDEN FISH

Having flown in from Singapore, a woman was arrested at Melbourne Airport in 2005 after customs officers heard "flipping and flapping noises from the vicinity of her waist." She had 51 live tropical fish in 15 water-filled bags attached to a purpose-built apron hidden under her skirt.

GRAPE TIME

Revellers frolic among grape pulp during the annual grape battle in Binissalem on the Spanish island of Mallorca. The town celebrates its wine tradition with the fiesta every year at the end of the grape festival.

TINY CONGREGATION

A wooden church in Drumheller, Alberta, is just 11 ft (3.4 m) long and 7 ft (2 m) wide. Originally built in 1968, Little Church has six one-person pews and a pulpit.

BANK PETS

Customers at the Union Federal Savings and Loan Bank in Kewanee, Illinois, can watch two otters, Andy and Oscar, romping in a climate-controlled play pool in the middle of the bank. They were introduced in 1991 by the bank's president.

FIRM BITE

Australian Rugby player Shane Millard was treated for an unusual head wound after a match. Doctors found a tooth from one of his opponents embedded in his skull.

FISH PARADE

The town of Aitkin, Minnesota, hosts an annual Fish House Parade. Fish houses (the sort used for ice fishing) are dressed in weird and wonderful themes and are paraded through town for eight blocks before thousands of enthusiastic spectators.

COFFIN FIT

Scotsman Alexander, Duke of Hamilton, spent more than £11,500 ($20,000) on a genuine ancient Egyptian coffin. But, when he died in 1852, he was found to be too long for it and so his legs had to be cut off before he could fit inside.

BODY SWAP

In 1876, an American gang of grave robbers tried unsuccessfully to steal Abraham Lincoln's body and hold it for ransom in return for the release of a convicted forger, Ben Boyd.

EXPLODING KING

When the body of King George IV of England became badly swollen in his coffin, court attendants feared that it would explode through the lining. So, they hurriedly drilled a hole in the casket to let out some of the rotten air.

DEAD WEIRD!

Wacky gravestones are all the rage in Japan. In a land where household altars and ornate headstones are the norm, specialist shops sell extraordinary-looking sculptures for remembering the dead. A gravestone shop in Fuji stocks such offbeat stone sculptures as Godzilla, a hippopotamus, and a baby dinosaur breaking through an egg. At a gravestone design competition in Japan in 2005, every taste was catered for, as shown below.

GLOW IN THE DARK

An Austrian company is selling solar-powered glow-in-the-dark gravestones. The grave appears normal during daylight hours, but once it gets dark it begins to glow. A family grave, large enough to hold 12 bodies, has already been constructed. The standard single version comes with a glowing gravestone, a solar roof, and a digital text display that allows relatives to program in names, the date of death, and personal blessings.

ACKNOWLEDGMENTS

FRONT COVER (c/l) Randy Finch/Derek Maxfield – ICEGURU.COM, (sp) George Whiteside; 4 (r) Randy Finch/Derek Maxfield – ICEGURU.COM; 5 (r) George Whiteside; 6 AP Photo/M. Spencer Green; 7 DPA Deutsche Press-Agentur/DPA/PA Photos; 12 Fredrik Schenholm/Ultimate Freedom Photography; 14 Petr Josek Snr/Reuters; 15 (t/l) Nora Pelyi/Rex Features, (r) Petr Josek Snr/Reuters; 16–17 Randy Finch/Derek Maxfield www.IceGuru.com; 18 Luray Caverns; 19 John Paul Brooke/Rex Features; 20 Simon Jones/Rex Features; 21 Lars Stroschen/Rex Features; 22–23 Solent News/Rex Features; 24–25 (dp) Scott Wishart/Rex Features; 25 (t) Photograph by Camera Press; 27 Action Press/Rex Features; 29 Hrywniak Bogdan/ABACA/PA Photos; 31 Sean Dempsey/PA Archive/PA Photos; 32–33 Reuters/John Gress; 37 Pacific Press Service/Rex Features; 38 Reuters/STR New; 40–41 Norm Betts/Rex Features; 42 Reuters/Yuriko Nakao; 43 George Whiteside; 44 (l) Reuters/Ho New, (r) Rex Features; 45 Reuters/Dani Cardona; 46 Masatochi Okauchi/Rex Features; 47 www.fuerrot.at/Rex Features

KEY t = top, b = bottom, c = center, l = left, r = right, sp = single page, dp = double page